If you play football, you need to be fit.

You can get fit too.

This is how.

You need to look at 4 top tips ...

1 You must train.

Jog and run.

Get fit. Don't get fat!

⭐ 2 Tuck into good food.

Don't pick rubbish food!

⭐3 Turn on the tap, not the fizz!

4 And get lots of rest, too!

So if you want to aim for the top …

get fit!